MY RHYMES. MY VOICE.

MUSIC

MY WAY!

BY ALI DACOSTA-PAUL

ILLUSTRATED BY DEMETRIUS FELDER-AGUIAR

For permission requests, please contact the publisher below:

Ali DaCosta-Paul
youngtalentedbyali@gmail.com
Baltimore, MD

www.Facebook.com/alidacostapaul

www.about.me/alidacostapaul

For information about special sales and purchases, please contact youngtalentedbyali@gmail.com

Cover Design by Derrick Barnes
Author photo by Aisha DaCosta-Paul
Interior book design by Derrick Barnes
Illustrated by Demitrius Felder-Aguiar
Edited by Aisha DaCosta-Paul

Library of Congress Control Number 2014905723

ISBN 978-0-615-99542-7

Printed in the United States of America

DEDICATION

This book is dedicated to every kid just like me that is filled with big dreams. You can do anything that you want to do if you work hard. Anything is possible.

My mom read a book that said music makes kids smarter. Even before I was born she wanted me to love music. When she was pregnant with me she even put headphones on her stomach and played Bob Marley songs for me to hear.

Maybe that's the reason why I have always loved music. Even as a little kid I used to sing along with every song on the radio.

When I turned eight years old, my mom decided that it was time for me to take music lessons. One day, she was talking to my uncle about which instrument I should learn to play. She said guitar because I was interested in it already. I even had a guitar in my room. My uncle suggested piano because he said it would make learning all other instruments easier.

My mom found a music studio that gave lessons in a lot of different instruments. They even had a kid's rock band. I was excited about my piano lessons. It sounded like fun.

Rocks for Kids
Instrument Room
Rock Band

My mom signed me up. Every Saturday, I had piano lessons for forty-five minutes.

At first, the lessons were cool. After a month of playing piano, I started to get bored. I didn't like all the rules to playing piano. I had to hold my hands a certain way. I had to play at a certain speed. It really started to drive me crazy.

are you Practicing???!!!

No! I am bored!!

I had homework from piano. I had to practice every day. When I didn't practice my mom would yell at me.

After the gazillionth time of my mother yelling at me about practicing piano, she finally asked if I liked it. I said, “No! I’m bored!” “Music is good for you!” mom said. “We have to find a way for you to love music again.”

studio CC
ok let's go!!

Best Rapper

My mom always comes up with these bright ideas. Sometimes, they are really out there. Sometimes, I don't even think she gets it. But, this time I think she had a really great idea. She told me that she asked a friend of hers, who was a local Hip-hop artist, to teach me how to rap. Although he never taught a kid how to rap before, he thought it was a cool idea and said he would give it a chance.

When we got to the studio for my first lesson I was very nervous. I loved listening to Hip-hop music but I wasn't sure if I would be good at it.

WHY LIE
LEGATO MUSIC

We got into the studio and I met my music teacher Mr. Young Ducki. He seemed like a cool guy. During my first lesson, he taught me about the studio equipment and the parts of a song.

My very first homework assignment was to write the hook and first verse of the song I would be recording. At first, I didn't know what I was doing. I wrote whatever came to my mind.Some of it was good. Some of it didn't make sense.

When I went back to the studio the next Saturday, Mr. Young Ducki asked, “So, what you got?” I read to him to what I wrote and he helped me say it to the beat.

Sometimes he would make me say the same words over and over again. Week after week, I would go to the studio to record another verse.Some weeks it was harder than others to find something to write about. When I got stuck, I would ask my mom for help. We would sit on the living room floor trading ideas until we found something that worked.

beats

It took four weeks of writing and recording to finish my first song, Swagged Out. Swagged Out is a story about a boy who is handsome with a great personality: basically, it is about me.

At the last recording session for Swagged Out I felt proud. I worked hard, asked for help when I was stuck.

I listened to the directions Mr. Young Ducki gave me. I created something that I didn't know was possible when I first started. I guess it is true that if you put good in, good will come out.

I really liked the freedom I had with my Hip-hop music lessons. Even though it was a lot of work, it allowed me to make music my way. I got a chance to be creative and use my voice. I want to make good music that helps people feel good about themselves.

In my song Swagged Out one of my favorite lines says, "Mirror, mirror on the wall. Asked him who's the greatest. He said, you the greatest of them all."

The message I am trying to say in this line is, that everyone can be the greatest if they put their heart and mind into everything they do.

you the greatest of them all!

I wrote what came to my mind. Sometimes when I was writing I didn't know where the song was going. That's what is cool about music. You really don't know what it is going to be until it is finished.

"My swag deeper than the ocean sea. Little mermaid can't see me. John Cena said he coming back. Make some room for the king of rap…" - *Swagged Out*

My mom was so excited about my first song that she told my teacher about it. My teacher listened to the song and decided to play it for the whole class.

Swagged out

Some of the kids in my class really liked it. They said things like, "Wow, that was great" and "I didn't know you had that talent in you". Other kids asked questions about how long I worked in the studio and if I had help.

"Don't judge a book by its cover. Believe in you. Believe in me. Believe in each other. They call me Ali, the world's eighth wonder. We all got talent to discover..."

- from my fourth song *Speakerphone*

As usual, there were haters that had negative comments. Some kid told me I was horrible at rapping. I told him, “then why don’t you do better?” There will always be haters. Use them as your motivators.

“Shout out to my haters. Ya’ll my motivators. Work hard. Play hard. Show them what you made of.”

- from my second song *Ali Bomaye*

Why don't you do better?

The word got out about my songs. It didn't take long for other teachers in my school to hear about them. At the school's Math Night, teachers were asking my mom for the link to my songs she had posted on the internet.

After five months of Hip-hop music lessons with Mr. Young Ducki, I have finished four songs. Sometimes, my mom plays my songs when we are riding in the car. I feel really proud hearing my music come through the car speakers.

My mom has shared my music with her friends and our family members.

Now, it's the first thing that they ask me about. It feels like I have my own fan club.

I think it is cool when you can make things that are boring more fun.

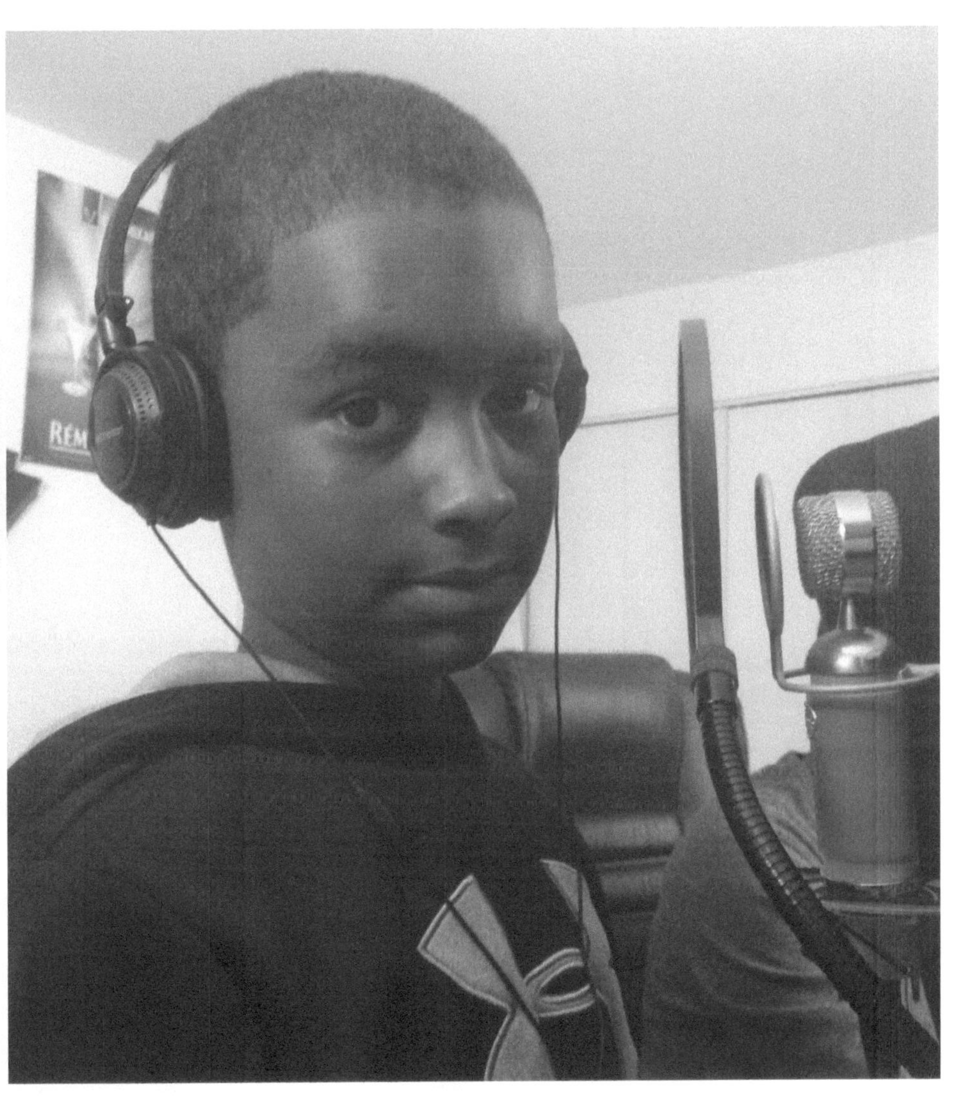

APPENDIX:
MY RHYMES

The first song that I wrote was Swagged Out. Swag is a slang word that is used as a noun, adjective, verb and all-purpose expression to label something or someone as cool or show approval.

SWAGGED OUT

Swag doesn't come from a box
People think it's easy but it's not
Life from above I should know
They say this is the life of the swag
They say shoes, money, cars
That's the way the world should be

Verse 1

Hop in the building
All eyes on me
Got the girls in love
And the boys trying to copy
My style (my style), my swag (my swag)
My walk (my walk), my flow (my flow)
Don't hate (don't hate), you know (you know)
I shine (I shine), I glow (I glow)
Swag like a firecracker
Lighting up in the sky
Fresher than water
Your style so dry
Be you and imma be me
I'm swagged out, the girl you like, she like me
(I'm swagged out, the girl you like she like me)

Chorus

My swag deeper than the ocean sea (deeper than the ocean sea)
Little Mermaid can't see me
John Cena said he coming back (coming back)
Make some room for the king of rap
Swagged out (swagged out) [x8]

Verse 2

Here's the difference between you and me
I don't fit in the crowd
The crowd fits to me
I'm swagged out (swagged out)
You got no doubt (no doubt)
There's more than the clothes
That make these people shout

Call me Mister Personality
Mirror, mirror on the wall
Ask him who the greatest
He say you the greatest of them all
Float like a butterfly
Sting like a bee
You better grab a bag
If you're trying to catch me
Hold up (hold up)

(Chorus)

Verse 3

Personality that'd be the key (that'd be the key)
Looking for a role model
Come see me (come see me)
Pictures this (picture this)
Living out my dreams
I'm crowd surfing (surfing til they scream)
Ali (Ali) you know who I be (I be)
I'm coast to coast
Hit me on my IG (IG)
In the studio
Putting in work (work)
Swagged out shorty I got Gucci on my shirt (shirt)

(Chorus)

Lyrics By: Ali Naysa Aamir DaCosta-Paul, Aisha D DaCosta, and Young Ducki Productions

My second song was Ali Bomaye. "Ali, Bomaye!" is a chant from Muhammad Ali and George Foreman's famous 1974 fight in Zaire (now Democratic Republic of Congo) called the Rumble in the Jungle.

Ali Bomaye

Chorus

Ali Bomaye
Man you betta say my name
Ali Bomaye
Man I'm about to change the game
Ali Bomaye
Say my name, say my name
Ali Bomaye (Ali Bomaye)
Ali Bomaye
Man you betta say my name
Ali Bomaye
Man I'm about to change the game
Ali Bomaye
Say my name, say my name
Ali Bomaye (Ali Bomaye)

Verse 1

Shout out to my haters
Ya'll my motivators
Work hard, play hard
Show 'em what you're made of
I'm chillin' on the block
I'm fresh, I'm fly
Ain't no future in frontin'
I ain't bragging I'm stuntin'
It ain't up for discussion
I ain't bragging I'm stuntin'
It ain't up for discussion (discussion)
Why lie, Work hard, Play hard
Gotta get your money
Show 'em what you're made of

Work so hard no payment
Ten push-ups on the pavement
Whistle blow and I can't quit
Exercise to get so fit
(Exercise to get so fit)
Man feel like I just can't quit

Get your weight up
Man you out classed
See me in the streets
Please no autographs
Please no autographs
And I got the people yelling they like

(Chorus)

Verse 2

Don't have it then go get it
Man I'm full of ambition
007 man I'm on a mission
Bball, Football, Rocking on a mic
Aint nothing wrong with wanting all three, alright!
I'm creating my reality
I can see it clearer
I see the man I wanna be
Looking in the mirror
Put a million on me
The brand is Ali
Work hard, play hard
Nothing comes free
Show em what I'm made of
Made of, made of
Shout out to my haters (haters)
Work so hard no payment
Ten push-ups on the pavement
Work so hard no payment (Ten push-ups on the pavement)

Man I represented
Shout out to my past
Shout out to my school
Cause I'm all about my math

Get your weight up
Man you out classed
See me in the streets
Please no autographs
Please no autographs
And I got the people yelling
They like

(Chorus)

Lyrics By: Ali Naysa Aamir DaCosta-Paul, Aisha D DaCosta and Young Ducki Productions

The third song that I wrote is called Ring the Alarm.

RING THE ALARM

Verse 1

I ain't waiting for your permission
Ten years red carpet admission
In 2020 I'm Lebron
With my face on the building
My sneakers on your feet
You and your children
Believe it before you see it man
That's what they call vision
Magic running through my veins
And I wanna live forever, Fame!
And ya'll gonna remember my name
(And ya'll gonna remember my name)

Put your shades on
Get ready for the light show
When I'm on the mic
Thermostat reaching inferno, Boom!
It's a fire in the building
One hot song now

Everybody feel him
Whooa!

I ain't trippin
I'm just living life
I'm just full of ambition
Trying to get it right
When I hit the studio
Make another song
You already know
They gonna
Ring the alarm

Chorus

Dial 911
Cause it's about to be on
Ring the alarm
Dial 911
Cause it's about to be on
Ring the alarm

Verse 2

People standing on they tippy toes
Screaming like I'm Michael Jackson
A living legend
Breath taken while
I'm taking action
Line up in an orderly fashion
Blazing like fire breathing dragon
They say talk is cheap
But my money still countin'
Ya'll sleep while I'm climbing up the mountain
I'm so hot
Fire no smoke
They call me Ali
I'm no joke
Step in the studio nearly choked
Getting money off the words that I quote
Being average man is something that I don't know

(Being average man is something that I don't know)
When I make it big
They'll gonna be like, I know him
Ask Kahlid, all I do is win, win, win
Riding 'round my side of town
Two chains with no chains
My music loud
That Novocain for dem ol' school days
I tell them ring the alarm

(Chorus)

Verse 3

An athlete, a rapper, a model, an actor
Going hard cause I never been a slacker
Mike Tyson knock out, first round
Man on the ground
Know he going down
Hip-hop ain't dead
Walking with the kings
You know I gotta dream
Ain't no "I" in team
Greatest of all time
Man, its Ali
You know who I be
No ID

(Chorus)

Lyrics By: Ali Naysa Aamir DaCosta-Paul, Aisha D DaCosta, and Young Ducki Productions

The last song that I recorded in 2013 was Speakerphone. We came up with the idea one day in the car. My mother was on the phone with a friend who started complaining about the call being on speakerphone.

SPEAKERPHONE

Chorus

Put me on your speakerphone
Turn me up
Let the world know
I'm ready for my close-up
Put me on your speakerphone
Can you hear me?
Turn me up

(repeat)

Verse 1

Batter up
I'm robbing first base
I wanna rock right now, Rob Base
I speak soft but
My words speak so loud (so loud)
Just tryna make my family proud

I'm in the zone
Eyes on the throne
I'm out of space
In a world of my own,
That's diggable
Don't judge a book by it's cover
Believe in you
Believe in me
Believe in each other

They call me Ali
The world's 8th wonder
We all got talent to discover

Burger King
You can have it your way
Teacher be like boy behave
I be like okay

(Chorus)

Verse 2

They say I'm lost in my head
Sleep walking
Following my dreams
Ain't nobody talking
Same ole, same ole
And it's getting' borin'
Wake me up
When they done
Cuz' I'm prolly snorin'

Leader of the new school
Show 'em how I'm livin'
I just hope they give back
Everything I'm givin'
Dreamin' (out loud)
Feels like a past life
Working hard
I ain't get no sleep
Last night
Beats by Ali
Running through your headphones
It's a party
I suggest
Don't leave this kid at home
I'm in my zone
Leave me alone
Let the world hear me
Put me on your speakerphone

(Chorus)

Verse 3

Charm City's favorite son
Talent amazing
I'm the one they talk bout
We know what you facing
From the harbor to the bay
They gonna say my name
Ali! Ali!
I'm just tryna win the game
Catch me on the radio
Mic check in the studio
Touchdown
Play it back
See me in the video
Knock Knock
Who's there?
Ali Ali
You already know
Who I be

(Chorus)

Lyrics By: Ali Naysa Aamir DaCosta-Paul and Aisha D DaCosta

www.ingramcontent.com/pod-product-compliance
Ingram Content Group UK Ltd.
Pitfield, Milton Keynes, MK11 3LW, UK
UKHW041849190726
13854UKWH00002B/793

9 780615 995427